GW01564231

Empath

25 Secrets to get your Sensitivity and Energy Under Control

Table of Contents

Introduction

The Struggles of an Empath

I want to thank you and congratulate you for buying the book, "*Empath: 25 Secrets to get your Sensitivity Under Control*".

What does the word "Empath" mean?

To be an empath means to be a highly sensitive personality type who can sense the emotions of others. Not only does it involve this ability, but it comes with the struggle of "taking on" other people's emotions, even if you don't particularly want to. As an empath, you feel everything in an extreme way, sensing the feelings of others with your intuition and emotion, rather than intellectually or logically. Empaths are naturally good at listening, giving, and being spiritually attuned. But it can be a struggle to be a person like this.

Empaths are no stranger to being told that they are "too sensitive" or should become tougher people. Situations and stimuli that seem to have no effect on others can leave you feeling very deeply, struggling hard to fit in socially, and even feeling foreign or alien, at times. Sometimes, you might pretend to not care at all, but if you're an empath, you always do. Perhaps you feel like you're flawed, wonder why you can't be like others, and wish desperately that you could. You might wish you were more accepted, or just wish to feel less, in general.

As an Empath, you Might find that...

- When other people walk around seemingly without a care in the world, not paying attention to others, you zone in on someone across the park who looks lonely, and feel their emotions deeply.

- When others receive criticism, it doesn't appear to bother them much, but you feel it strongly and spend time thinking about it over and over in the following days.

- While other people can attend parties, have fun and mingle without a care, you look for a restroom to gather your thoughts in and try to get your energy under control.

- When other people stand up for themselves, you have a hard time learning how to say "no" and have a tendency to put the needs of others before your own happiness, or even sanity.

Once you discover the word "empath", you may experience an entire new understanding and freedom. You realize that you are not foreign to the world or an alien, you're just highly empathetic. If the points above resonated with you and you found yourself nodding along, chances are you are also an empath. This book is intended to help you navigate life, protect yourself, and control your sensitivity so that you can live to the fullest. In this book, we are going to help you figure out whether you are sensitive and empathetic, or a full on empath (yes there's a difference and it's important) in the first chapter. The following chapters will give you tips for dealing with it positively and healthily.

Thanks again for buying this book, I hope you enjoy it!

Chapter 1

How to tell if you're an Empath vs. Empathetic

On the surface, these two might sound like the same thing, but they are actually different. Most people have empathetic tendencies, at least to some degree, but not everyone is a full-on empath. It's important to recognize whether you are simply highly sensitive or are an empath, since each personality type calls for different methods for handling it.

Are you Empathetic or an Empath?

If you are highly sensitive by nature, it's likely that you also identify with having high levels of empathy. You might even prefer this term to the notion of being "highly sensitive." Being someone who is empathetic simply refers to being able to relate to the way others feel, so what is the difference between this and being an actual empath? Well, "empath" is another word for having clairsentience. This means that you simply "know" things that others don't know. This means that we are moving into the world of spirituality, which lies beyond psychology. Although up to 20 percent of the world's population is highly sensitive, only up to 4 percent is actually clairsentient.

What's the Actual Difference and Why does it Matter?

If you're still wondering what other differences there are, it's not so easy to answer in clear cut terms, but there are some people who are highly sensitive and also fit the empath category. There are others who are highly sensitive (and empathetic) but don't fit the actual empath category, and others who lie somewhere in between. This causes lines to get blurred quite easily, and can cause confusion. The important question here is why is this distinction important, or why does it really matter?

- **Training and Knowledge:** One reason why the distinction is important is because if you're an empath, having certain knowledge and training is almost needed in order to use your abilities without becoming mentally frazzled, emotionally exhausted, or just overwhelmed in general.

- **Labels can Help:** In addition, labels can be helpful, at times. Labels are important because they simplify the idea of receiving understanding and support. When you understand yourself, you can better relate to others and explain the way you are to them. Everyone exists within a mix of random categories and labels, which makes it important to know what is what when you talk about them. Once you understand these aspects of yourself, it's easier to figure out what you truly need from life to be happy and fulfilled. It's all part of the process of growing and maturing into a full person.

- **Acknowledging Abilities:** Another important reason to know the difference between high sensitivity and being an actual empath is the fact that you are denying the empath's abilities when you only see them as sensitive. There is much more to it than that. Accepting that you are simply sensitive is tempting because it's a familiar term, and not as uncommon. It's simpler to just accept that you are good at reading expressions, paying attention to nonverbal cues and body language, and imagining what it would be like to be someone else.

This is easier than accepting that you have very strong abilities to intuit information about others that transcends the realm of "normal." When you are simply sensitive, you are working within an accepted model of psychology and a particular personality profile that has been studied. That makes the process more comfortable, because you can pinpoint the reasons for being the way you are, such as your differently structured nervous system. However, denying your empath nature means being cut off from your abilities, and without acknowledging these gifts, you can't make use of them.

Some people who fall into the "empath" or "highly empathetic person" category are fine with this, and find that their lives end up naturally falling into place. Others, however, might struggle with fitting in, particularly making their emotions and concept of being an empath fit with their current worldviews, academic life, or religious beliefs. This might end up synthesizing into something healthy and wonderful, over time, but at others, it can be a painful struggle. This book is an attempt to acknowledge all of your natural gifts, even the ones that you haven't recognized yourself yet.

Your Worldview and Accepting being an Empath:

There are some ways in which your worldview has to shift in order to make way for your nature as an empath, but how so?

- Energy is not only a useful metaphor, but something that exists in a real way and can be perceived with your senses on a physical level.

- Physical sensations and emotions are very real energy that shifts from person to person, and you are especially sensitive to noticing it.

- Energy is thrown around, can stick to you, be handed to someone else, and even blend in with other people's energies.

What is Obsession like for an Empath?

In terms of traditional psychological models, all of the above is simply symbolic ideas, but to an empath, this is extremely real, and not acknowledging that can have serious consequences. When you are an empath and you obsess about someone else, this is not only happening in your mind, but shows that energy exchanges are happening on a subconscious level with that person. If you notice that you deeply impacted by another person, you are not simply putting yourself in their shoes or empathizing, but literally reading their energies. In what ways is that different than the typical obsession people get over each other?

- **Obsession for a Sensitive Person:** For a person who is merely sensitive, an attention shift or having a conversation with another person is enough to wake them up from the obsession. Although letting go isn't always easy, taking a psychological or rational approach does work wonders.

- **Obsession for an Empath:** But when you are entangled in an obsession with someone as an empath, it doesn't matter how much you change your mind, talk about it, or attempt to let the thoughts go, there is still something there nagging you. Even if you go through all of the steps necessary to forget about it and move on with your life, you still struggle and get stuck.

This is because it's not a matter of simply thinking of a person, you are actually absorbing their energies and have to think about it from that perspective, rather than simply a psychological perspective. This can apply to many different situations, but it's particularly strong when it comes to specific people. That is precisely why training yourself as an empath matters, it gets specific and transcends the models of psychology for protecting yourself and staying healthy.

Energy as a Sensitive Person vs. an Empath:

Highly sensitive people are proven to respond more sensitively and intensely to outside stimuli, and empaths can't help but react to the energy of other people more intensely. The wiring of a highly sensitive person is psychological and biological, while the wiring of an empath is psychological and energetic in nature, having real effects on the body. This means that while thinking of yourself as an empath, you must think in terms of energy to fully understand how you work. If you still aren't certain about whether you are an empath or not, you can check out the list below to get a clearer understanding.

Signs that you are an Unidentified or Untrained Empath:

Below is a list of scenarios or situations that are probably familiar to you if you are either unidentified or untrained as an empath. Keep in mind that experienced and trained empaths will likely not relate to teach list item. Read each item over and see if it applies to you:

- **Concentration:** You find it difficult to focus or concentrate when you're around most other people, because you keep feeling their presence, emotions, or various moods, but when you're alone this isn't a problem at all.

- **Relief:** People have often told you that they feel relief after being around you or talking to you about their problems (either emotional or physical), even though you often feel worse during these times.

- **Changing Moods:** If you're around a lot of different people, your physical or emotional feelings change a lot, and quite quickly. You may even feel as though you're going crazy, but once you are alone again, you feel fine.

- **Feeling the Pain of Others:** You have noticed pains or aches, or strong feelings that came from nowhere, and found out later on that a loved one was experiencing that same pain.

- **Taking on Troubles:** You experience the troubles of others as though they were yours, and in a way you take responsibility for their wellbeing. Even if you realize that this is not necessarily healthy, it's very hard to untangle yourself from this instinct.

- **Slow Emotional Recovery:** You take way longer than other people to recover from an emotionally intense situation, like being yelled at. In addition, it might take you longer to recover from emotional trauma, such as losing someone you love.

- **Discomfort from Others:** Some people don't feel comfortable around you because they think that you can see into them or through them.

- **Sensing Personality Traits:** You can immediately sense if someone is shy, comfortable, sensitive, artistic, or hardened simply by looking at them and the way they interact with their environment. Oftentimes, you can sense this without ever speaking to them or hearing them speak.

- **Acting unlike yourself:** You've noticed that when you're with some people, you feel, act, or think in a way that is not like you. When they aren't around anymore, you feel normal again. It can be easy to think of yourself as weak or impressionable for this reason.

- **Trouble Identifying your Needs:** Although noticing the wants and needs of other people seems to come without effort to you, knowing your own is much harder. In order to find out, you have to spend time alone, and this doesn't always lead to a resolution or answer.

- **Trouble with Disappointing others:** Dealing with causing others grief or anger is very difficult for you, and it's almost impossible to handle letting someone down. For this reason, it's tough to set boundaries with others because you fear their negative responses.

- **Unexplained Discomfort:** You oftentimes feel dark or icky for no apparent reason, almost like being sick, but different. You prefer to distract yourself mentally from your body for this reason.

- **Picking up on Intoxication:** When you are around intoxicated people, you can pick up on their state of mind. For example, if you're in a drunk group of people, but haven't had any alcohol yourself, you can end up feeling drunk, as well.

- **Eye Contact is Intense for you:** Being close to someone or making direct eye contact with them can be an overwhelming impact on you emotionally, especially if they are in the throes of an intense mood.

Keep in mind that the above points are only general points that you could recognize if you have not trained or identified yourself as an empath yet. The only way to know for sure is to keep reading to see if the rest of the signs and secrets in the book apply to you. Remember that the signs listed above don't necessarily mean that you are an empath, but if you are, suffering doesn't need to come with it. All it takes is a willingness to learn more about your nature, and the knowledge and ability to work with, rather than against, it. Once you commit to becoming proficient in handling this trait, you will be able to confidently deal with situations that you would have only avoided before.

Chapter 2

Getting your Energy under Control

Being highly sensitive is completely normal, and these personality types make up at least 15 percent of the global population. Being an empath means that you automatically relate to those who are highly sensitive, and they will probably understand you better than most, as well. As an empath, you are constantly aware of the subtleties around you, noticing the little details that others would never see. This means that you get overwhelmed much more easily, if you don't know how to control this trait. It's only logical, since noticing everything leads to reacting more strongly to novel, chaotic, complex, or intense situations, especially if they are long lasting.

Being Mistaken for a Neurotic Person:

Being an empath is something that is highly misunderstood, because you tend to take your time with situations. For this reason, you might be labeled as shy or introverted. While many empaths do have these traits, it isn't necessarily always the case. Shyness is something that you learn to be, it isn't something you are born with such as intense empathy. The gifts of an empath are valued in some cultures, and completely denied in others. For this reason, empaths often struggle with their self-image and levels of self-esteem, feeling abnormal. As an empath, you likely feel as though your personal space is being invaded almost constantly by surrounding feelings and energy of other people. This can be draining and exhausting if you don't take the proper measures to protect yourself.

Using the 25 Secrets for getting your Sensitivity Under Control:

This is the point of the secrets you are about to learn. The key here is to use every single secret given to you in this book and stick to the ones that work best for you. Your natural sense of giving and heightened senses are great gifts that can help you and the rest of the world. If you wield them right, you have a lot of power and can help others in amazing ways, including yourself. If you use your powers of being an empath wrongly, however, you might lose them or end up lost. Keep trying out different methods, and even combinations of the methods in this book, until you find your perfect routine and program for handling your personal sensitivity.

Secret Number One: Handling Invaded Personal Space.

As an empath, you probably appreciate your space, which can make it overwhelming when others don't respect or acknowledge that. So next time someone is getting a bit too close to you (either mentally, emotionally, or physically) and you can't find a way to escape, follow these steps to stay grounded and anchored to your inner strength:

- **Plant yourself:** The first step is to plant both of your feet firmly to the floor or the ground, ideally without any shoes on. You can press them down hard and even wiggle the toes a bit. This will give you the psychological benefit and effect of feeling grounded in your body and on earth. We've all found ourselves in the situation of encountering someone's anger or negative emotions, without the ability to leave, so this anchor can keep you centered.

- **Remind:** Next you should try reminding yourself that the earth is below you giving you full support, enabling you to hold on instead of getting swept downstream in a strong current of emotion. Our planet is stronger than us and our feelings, no matter how overwhelming they can seem at any given moment in time. You might have your attention on the individual who is unloading their feelings onto you, but focus your awareness on the ground you're standing on, and draw strength from it.

If you find yourself moving toward a situation or person that is emotionally overwhelming or overbearing, try to notice every step you're taking. When your feet hit the floor or ground, walk in a harder way than you normally would. This might make your feet feel as though they weigh more than usual, like they are carrying weights. When you focus on the ground with your feet, you are tapping into your own energy, rather than the energies around you. This is a valuable skill in an emotionally overbearing reality.

Secret Number Two: Using Triggers for Finding your Energy Again.

As empaths, we are no strangers to getting swept away by other people's energies. In order to bring yourself back to a calm place, you can touch your fingertips together (such as your pointer finger and thumb) or physically hold or touch a calming object, like a talisman or touchstone.

- **A Significant and Calming Object:** This differs for everyone, but your object could be jewelry, a special coin, a stone, or crystal, but it has to be small enough to carry on your person at all times. The easiest anchor to create for this is simply touching your fingertips together. Your fingertips are always there, and they can remind you that you are real. You are one inhabiting your body and therefore, your emotions are the only ones that you should be in control of or worried about.

- **Remind yourself that you're in Control**: This helps you remember that you're the one in control here, not other people. Oftentimes, as an empath, you don't feel as real as others, because your feelings have been taken over by someone else's, leading you to lose your control over yourself and get swept up in the other person. You may even have a hard time telling the difference between their emotions and yours. When you touch your object or even just your fingertips together, it can put you back into the drive seat of your existence.

This will remind you that you are the center of your world, no one else is. Some find it helpful to use something called mudras, which are hand gestures present in Hinduism and Buddhism. This is especially helpful if you are spiritual or religious.

Secret Number Three: Getting into your Body.

Empaths are used to getting so overwhelmed by emotions (both theirs and the emotions of other people) that it leads them to feel anxiety or even, in serious situations, end up shaking. The best way to combat this is to get moving. Do some kick boxing, go for a run, do yoga or jumping jacks, or something else that gets your blood flowing and your body in motion. Why does this work?

- **Emotions are Energy:** As mentioned earlier in the book, emotions are just energy within us, and for empaths (deep feelers), it has a stronger effect on us physically. This could lead to shaking when you are upset, anxious, or scared. At times, there can be such a high level of energy going through you that your body is overwhelmed and it leads to crying or trembling. This is how your body releases the excess energy inside of you.

- **Exercising helps to Release it**: When you're in the throes of a strong emotion, you can help yourself release the excess energy of emotion by doing some intense exercise. Even if you only jump around for a minute or two, this helps a lot, or you could do something longer and more intense like a hard sprint outside. Whenever you decide to move around intentionally, you are allowing this energy to have a route to escape your body. For some, this outlet is dance, for others, it's punching a bag a few times. Find what works for you!

Secret Number Four: Let your Emotions Flow.

As empaths, our emotions are often so strong that we are afraid to let them run wild. It seems as though something crazy, wild, or uncontrollable might happen if we do. But what if this is part of the problem?

- **Acknowledge:** Next time you get this urge, try to let the emotions flow through you freely, instead. Start by acknowledging that the feelings are there inside of your mind and heart. Most empaths have a necessity to have some type of shield around them for protection against intense emotions outside of us. Although this has its time and place, and can be a valuable tool (which we will go into more later), it's not always necessary.

- **Embrace:** After acknowledging your feelings and allowing them to freely flow throughout your being, you can start visualizing a bright white light around your body, protecting you from outside harm. As you learn to recognize your own strength to overcome hardships, this may become less necessary, but it's a good tool for when you're feeling overwhelmed. Eventually, you will come to realize that your unique sensitivity is, in fact, a gift, and not a curse. Until then, use protection when you need it, and let your emotions flow at other times.

So, the next instance you have of feeling an intense emotion rushing toward you, breathe deeply and just let it happen. Imagine yourself as a conduit that the energy can flow through unobstructed. When you don't put up any resistance, you allow the feelings to freely go through you, washing through your being and body and leaving just as quickly. There's no need to analyze, dissect, criticize, or judge the emotions, just allow them to be and release them.

Secret Number Five: What is Happening inside?

One of the best habits you can get into is the habit of asking yourself what is happening inside you throughout the day. This simple but powerful question gets you back on track and heading the right way. Instead of trying to analyze your own thoughts and feelings, adopt a curious and observant position instead. Place your full attention within yourself, feeling every nuance of energy in your emotions. If you don't feel any emotions at the moment, simply try to focus on the physical field of energy in the body, which can lead you to a relaxed, calm, and present state of mind.

- **Emotions as Thought Patterns:** Your feelings typically represent some type of energized and amplified pattern of thought. Due to the fact that these can be overwhelming and overpowering when we feel them, it's hard to stay conscious and calm enough to pay attention to what's happening in your body. But all trained empaths who are in control of their own sensitivity have learned how to do this, and you can too. The strong emotion and attachment to negative thoughts want to take over your mind, and it often happens, but when you stay present and centered, observing instead of judging, you can fight this vicious cycle.

- **When you Identify with the Emotion:** If you do get swept up by the emotion and come to identify with it unconsciously, and do not remain present (completely normal and common), then your emotions become "you" for the time being. This then starts a circle between your emotions and thoughts, which feed and support each other. This pattern of thought then creates an even larger reflection as an emotion, feeding the pattern of thought. Then it's tempting to swell on whatever situation is "causing" the reaction, energizing the cycle even further.

An example of this is when you're driving in traffic and someone cuts you off. You feel a strong surge of annoyance within you. Then the thought comes to justify the annoyance, "How could that driver have been so careless and stupid?" which only fuels your emotional state even further. When you are in a negative cycle like this, you are drawing more and more negativity towards you, and before you even know it, you've been sucked into a bad mood which might even ruin your entire day.

You can break this cycle by making it a habit to notice what is happening inside of you many times throughout the day. Remember not to judge yourself for what you see, which is the hardest part. Pay attention to the times when you feel at peace, or annoyed, or even frustrated. You can stay on top of your emotional states simply by noticing them when they are there. Like any other worthwhile skill, this will take time to practice, but it's well worth it.

Self-Esteem for the Empath Personality Type:

For reasons we have already discussed in earlier sections of the book, such as taking on the energy of others, not realizing how your own thoughts and feelings work, and taking responsibility for the feelings of others, it's common that empaths struggle with their own self-worth. To put it simply, a healthy sense of self-esteem must include feeling okay with who you are, and feeling comfortable in your skin. But empaths who are not yet trained to handle their own traits and abilities have already taken on so much of the energy of other people that it has become embedded into their sense of self, causing discomfort, both physically and mentally.

The Importance of your own Mental and Emotional Health:

It isn't very easy to feel good in life or about your personality when you feel bad physically. You may mistakenly believe that your feelings are uncontrollable and have no idea what you can do to help fix it. This could lead you to spiral downward into self-deprecating or even hateful thoughts. You might try to help others as a way to combat this depression or increase your self-worth, but without taking care of yourself first, this will only make matters worse. Until you learn to first make sure you are okay, you can't truly help others with your unique gifts. For that reason, you must follow the secrets in this book to make sure you're on the right, healthy track as an empath.

Chapter 3

Crying, and Identifying your Drains and Triggers

If you have found your way to this book and read this far, chances are you are most definitely an empath. You probably knew you were after researching the term a little bit. The realization that there is an actual term for who you are and your "condition" likely brought a lot of relief and understanding. At last you can make sense of why you have always felt different, why you appear to be more sensitive than nearly everyone else, and why different people and places affect you so strongly and strangely. The empath personality type is an inquisitive mind which enjoys getting confirmation for their hunches, suspicions, or strong intuitive feelings. Hopefully this chapter will provide you with more satisfying insight into why you are the way you are, and how you should handle it from this point forward.

Knowing, Feelings, and Overwhelm:

The empath type of person simply knows things without having to be told them. This is a type of knowing that transcends gut feelings or even intuition, but some describe it using these terms since it's the only words we've been given. The better attuned you are with yourself and your knowing, the more certain you become of your knowing, and the stronger it gets. You are, as an empath, way too familiar with the idea of getting really overwhelmed in public places, including crowded stadiums, concerts, malls, or even grocery markets. This is because you are being bombarded with emotions everywhere you turn and might not have even realized it.

Feeling the emotions of those around you and mistaking them as your personal feelings is just a part of this personality type, and something you get used to with time. You might even recognize that someone is judging you, feeling sad, or insecure from a far distance. With the right knowledge, tips, and the secrets in this book, you will no longer be thrown out of whack every time this happens to you.

Secret Number Six: Accept that Crying is Fine.

This is a very important one; you need to allow yourself to cry. It's completely okay, and a very human thing to do. You might feel like crying when you get happy, when you are disappointed, when something moves you, or even when you see a cute bunny rabbit. You might find that you have tears just waiting there to come out at the slightest stimuli.

- **A Natural Release:** Many of us have a resistance to crying. It might be because we've been trained and conditioned to act tough, to not show the world that something bothers us, or simply because we don't like to answer questions about what's bothering us. But this is an unhealthy and limiting perspective to hold onto. Crying is a good thing, and it's the way your body lets go of extra emotions that need release.

- **Learn to Like it:** You should teach yourself to appreciate crying for what it is, whether it's happy or sad tears you're experiencing. It can be a wonderful state of flow and release for you, when viewed the right way. Especially as an empath, making use of this natural human function is a great asset to have. Allow yourself to have a session of crying every so often. When your body feels like crying, it's because you need to.

Even when you're in a situation that doesn't seem like a "big deal", you should cry when you get the urge to cry. All of us go through life accumulating resentments and conflicts, and this is even stronger for the empath. There is nothing weak about this at all, and crying is the most cathartic activity we can ever engage in. It allows the devils in your system to get out before they can cause true harm on your physical and mental systems.

Secret Number Seven: Wake up Earlier.

Too often, people live as though they are never going to die. When you lose someone in your life, or go through some type of trauma, you suddenly realize that life is not something to take for granted. Although it may sound cliché, it's usually something devastating that brings along this realization in full force. And although many of us may "know" this on some level, not everyone actually does anything about it. We are all aware that life is fleeting and precious, but we act like it's never going to end, wasting our time watching television or hating our jobs.

- **Changing your Schedule:** Every empath or sensitive person in general should adjust their schedule so that they have some quiet time to themselves in the mornings. This will give you a new level of clarity, energy, and productivity. When you wake up earlier, you have time to yourself and can get yourself into the frame of mind you need to be in before you take on your day.

- **Quiet time is Important:** For someone who soaks up their surroundings and all of the emotions of other people, quiet time in the morning to get into a calm state of being is an absolute necessity Once you start doing it, you will wonder how you ever survived without it. During this time, your time is yours and no one else's. This is a good chance to listen to music, journal, meditate, or just relax and gather your thoughts quietly and peacefully.

Instead of jumping right onto the internet to check your email like most of us do every morning, spend some time slowly entering your day. Use this time to get connected with yourself mentally, emotionally, and on a spiritual level. Some might like to go for a run or do some yoga, others might wish to read something inspiring. What you do with this time is up to you.

Secret Number Eight: Identifying your Triggers.

Part of navigating life and thriving as an empath is knowing what it is what sets you off, both in a positive and negative way. This involves identifying both the situations that drain your energy and the situations that enhance it or add to it.

- **Draining Situations:** This could be anything from obvious triggers (crowded places or encountering an angry person) to more subtle ones (such as reading a sad story on the internet or seeing something on television that makes you feel bad.) The best way to find out what your triggers are is to start taking notes on your emotional state of mind throughout the day. You could also do a review at the end of each day, trying to recall moments that you felt overwhelmed, emotionally exhausted, or otherwise negative.

- **Energizing Situations:** Just as important as identifying your negative and draining triggers is figuring out what energizes you. This could be certain people that you see, such as friends at work or specific family members, or seeing something funny. It could also be something as simple as looking at cat pictures on the internet. Figure out what it is that makes you feel strong, happy, and emotionally centered.

- **The People in your Life:** The people you spend time with on a daily or weekly basis play a huge role in your state of mind, whether you realize it or not. Some people lift us up and leave us feeling good about ourselves, while others make us feel emotionally sick. This is important to pay attention to, especially as an empath. It can be hard to limit time with certain people, such as co-workers or family members, but whenever possible, you should try to fit your schedule around spending time with positive influences, instead of negative ones that pull you down.

As soon as you figure out your emotional triggers, you can start re-structuring your life to fit what you found out. With this new knowledge, you can start to stay away from draining situations and gravitate toward positive ones, instead. This might sound like a simple step, and it can be, but controlling the flow of your emotions via your environment gives you an extra boost in taking back the reigns of your own life.

Secret Number Nine: Creating a Protective Shield.

Although staying strong, or as we mentioned in another tip, letting your emotions flow, are positive strategies, at times you need a protective shield. There are always certain situations that require you, as an empath, to withstand even if you would rather run as far as you can away from them. This could be work related situations, family functions, or other social situations that come with energies or people that are hard for you to handle or be around. Since doing things we don't want to do is just a part of life sometimes, and necessary, you must figure out ways to cope with these circumstances. A shield of energy is one such method for this.

- **Visualize:** Start by visualizing your protective shield. This could be a bubble that encases your entire body, or a bright light that washes over you whenever you need it to. Inside of that barrier, nothing can harm you. Although this seems like simple imagination, visualizations like this actually have powerful effects and results in your life and confidence.

- **Practice:** Try putting up this protective bubble, light, or shield when you don't need it at first, so that you get good at calling it to mind whenever it's needed. A good time to practice this is in idle or calm moments such as first waking up, falling asleep, or even taking a shower or driving to work.

- **Use it:** Now that you are used to practicing this and using it at will, you can put it up whenever you need it. Whenever you can sense that your emotional energies are about to be compromised or drained by people or a certain situation, you can stop this in its tracks by putting up your personal protective shield.

Secret Number Ten: Pay Attention to the Source of your Feelings and Thoughts.

If you have a hard time building up a bubble or shield to keep away negative feelings and thoughts, you can start with watching your mental processes to figure out where they are coming from.

- **Find the Original Source:** You might, for example, notice that you are feeling angry. This is a good chance to find out whether it's your anger or whether you "caught" it from someone else. As soon as you can identify the source of that feeling, you can start to look for a way to fix it.

- **Find the Message behind the Feeling:** Every feeling has a message behind it, or a reason why it exists. Figure out what your emotion is saying to you. It could be that you think there is something missing or that you don't like the way someone else is acting. Figure out what this feeling is pointing you toward. It could be anything from a few quiet moments to yourself to a talk with another person.

- **Take Action:** An important part of releasing emotion is taking actual action to resolve it. This can be something as simple as taking a walk or talking yourself through something. The important part is that you recognize what is needed and you deliver it.

Why can being an Empath be so Confusing?

There are a few different reasons why it can be struggle to have this type of personality. One main reason is that having the abilities you have calls for a radical shift in your world views.

- **A Lack of Quality Information or Understanding:** Since there isn't much general information or understanding on the way this ability functions, you might find yourself without tools to make sense of it. At the very least, you have likely gone through years of your life this way before realizing what your answers and solutions were. On that note, hopefully this book is providing you with some.

- **The Confusion of Soaking up Others' Emotions:** Some empaths, even the ones who are familiar with their personality type and think of themselves as experienced, don't actually know how much of their emotions have been absorbed from other people. This happens mainly because awareness does not exist around what is happening, which isn't very surprising. It gets confusing because we are taught that what we feel is our own emotion. If someone feels sadness, they are sad, which sounds simple and obvious. However, when you're an empathy, the sadness you feel might not be your own at all.

Even when you notice that some of your feelings aren't necessarily your own feelings, you might still get confused what you got from others and what naturally came about within yourself. It isn't only what you're sensing around you at this very moment that is significant, but the opinions and feelings of other people that impacted you in the past, as well. This effect can be so strong that you might believe you want something or have a certain opinion, when it was only passed to you from an outside source years back. It's easy to assume that what you feel is because it's what you're feeling, but this is only one possible layer of the equation.

Figuring out what feelings are yours and what feelings belong to other people takes training and awareness. It can be tempting to fall into a trap where you use the excuse that your feelings are not your own as a way to avoid dealing with them at all. You must learn some techniques that help you figure it out in every individual situation. Some of the techniques in the following chapter should be helpful in this area.

Chapter 4

Forgiveness and Positive Affirmations

When you're an empath, you tend to be a great listener, often without having to try. You don't usually talk much about yourself unless you're with a person that you have a lot of trust in. Instead your caring nature and love of learning helps you keep open ears for people that want to share things with you. But not everyone is pleasant for you to be around. When you are around someone who is very harsh, egotistical, or narcissistic, it can be almost painful. Another common pain of the empath is shifting moods. At times, you might feel very disconnected and moody, while at other times, you're the bubbliest person in the world.

Being Genuine is a Must for the Empath:

In our society, it's often considered polite to act happy even when you aren't, or to be nice to someone even if you would rather not. For the empath, however, this is unbearable. You need to have the freedom to express your emotions and to be around people who can accept that you aren't happy all the time (and no one is.) For this reason, you might find customer service jobs quite challenging. Whatever challenges your life brings you, however, there's a way to handle it. Let's get on to the seventh secret for having control over your sensitivity.

Secret Number Eleven: Use Positive Affirmations.

Empaths are typically very giving and open individuals, but positivity is not always easy when you soak up the emotions of others constantly. Due to their ability to feel the world and people around them, empaths may suffer grief and sadness that came from a source outside of themselves. In order to remain positive, you should utilize positive affirmations. Here are the guidelines for success with this secret:

- **Write down your Goals:** What do you wish to change in your life? If you want to feel more confident in your own skin, your affirmation should be, "I am self-assured in everything I do." You must speak as though what you want is already true. This will train your subconscious to believe it's true and act as though it is. Make a couple of themed affirmations to start with that focus on one general area of self-improvement.

- **Repeat them Aloud:** Next, you should stand in the mirror and say these affirmations aloud to yourself for at least five minutes at a time. This might feel strange or awkward at first, but it will get easier and feel more natural as you get used to it. You should do this a minimum of once a day (in the morning), but ideally twice a day (the mornings and evenings, before bed.)

- **Be Consistent:** Affirmations only work if you are faithful and consistent with your practice. Essentially what you are trying to do is retrain your subconscious mind to have different beliefs, so this takes time and effort. Think about the subconscious beliefs you hold now, how long did those take to form and stick? Probably quite a while, so put the dedication into this that it deserves and enjoy the results!

Within two weeks, you should notice drastic changes in your life directly from doing these affirmations. Keep in mind that the phrases you use must be positive, such as "I walk with poised confidence," rather than negative, such as, "I want to stop slouching." This way, you are telling your subconscious mind what you *do* want, not what you don't want.

Secret Number Twelve: Get Grounded.

You might discover that, being an empath personality, you actually have a natural strong connection with this planet than others. This can be used to your advantage, as long as you know how to do it. This is similar to the secret we gave you in the first chapter about planting your feet firmly into the ground, but also different. It's perfectly possible for you to take negative energies and emotions you are feeling and "give" them to, or allow them to be absorbed into, the earth. In a similar way, this connection can provide you with healthy and positive energies. Strengthen this existing bond by spending a lot of time outside enjoying and appreciating nature, and consistently think on your connection with the earth as you walk on it, throughout the day.

Secret Number Thirteen: Practice Forgiveness.

True forgiveness is a (sometimes difficult) process in which bad or painful energies have been stored within you and you allow them to be released. This might be a particular person or event that happened to you in the past, but the longer you grasp onto this, the more it will continue to suck away your energy. You have to detach yourself from these painful associations so that you can heal. Being someone who is very sensitive, you might discover that you get hurt more easily than others, which is a natural product of being so caring. Learning how to forgive people is very important for emotional health.

Secret Number Fourteen: Emotional Catharsis.

- **The Harm of Storing Emotions:** Empaths usually have lively and busy mental landscapes that wrestle and try to handle countless feelings that come at them throughout the day. This can lead to them becoming so involved and stuck in their own heads that they forget to purge and process those emotions, storing them away and allowing them to affect them continuously.

- **Letting Emotions through:** Catharsis allows you to feel your strongest emotions and expressing them for what they are. This can mean yelling when angry, laughing when you're amused, or crying when you get frustrated. All of these are genuine expressions, and can be positive outlets for you. There is nothing wrong with letting emotions come up as they want to, as long as you aren't harming others in the process.

- **Find your Outlet:** Once you have gotten into the habit of letting your emotions exist within you and show, find a positive outlet for expressing them. This can be music, art, or even a sport.

Secret Number Fifteen: Schedule Time to yourself.

Most of the secrets given to you in this book require time by yourself, which makes it necessary for you to find and schedule plenty of alone time for yourself to practice them. This might involve saying no to some friends who wish to see you, or even disappointing family members, but don't forget that your own happiness is important too and must be covered before you can give anything to others. Plus, if you want your loved ones to see your best, you have to make sure you're healthy and taken care of. Here are some ideas for activities you can do while you are having some time to yourself:

- **Meditation:** Meditation is a great way to calm yourself when you're stressed out, or even just to use as an avenue for getting to know yourself more. If you don't know how to meditate, you can use some guided meditations on YouTube, or simply follow these instructions. Find a quiet place to sit where you will not be disturbed by any noise. Sit cross legged (or in a straight backed chair if this is more comfortable for you) and close your eyes. Start to breathe deeply and focus on your breathing. Thoughts will start to cross your mind, which is okay.

Let the thoughts come into your mind and leave again without any stress. You will have to continuously pull your mind back to your breath, before it becomes a habit. Others might find it more helpful to stare at something, such as a candle flame or wall, instead of keeping their eyes closed. Whenever you sit down to meditate, set your timer for at least 10 minutes, so you have some structure. Try to do this at least once a day. Meditation is proven to have many physical and mental benefits, so it's a good time to start!

- **Art:** I am a firm believer in the fact that everyone is creative, even if they don't know it. If you're an empath, chances are, you already have an art form that you regularly practice. On the off chance that you don't, this is something that you should definitely get into. Whether you have always been curious about sculpture building, or you've been wanting to learn how to knit for a while, follow what interests you. This is a great way to reconnect with yourself and get mentally and spiritually healthy.

- **Walking:** Walking is a great way to clear your head, come up with ideas or solutions to issues that have been bothering you, or simply a nice way to get some time to yourself. The average American citizen doesn't get enough exercise, and this is very bad for you on a mental level. Make it a point to get outside at least once a day for a minimum of 15 minutes, whether it's scorching hot or there's snow falling outside. Not only will your body thank you, but you'll feel better mentally, as well.

- **Spending Time with Animals:** Most empaths connect naturally and deeply with animals. In fact, some of them relate better to animals than their fellow humans. If this is the case for you, spending time with animals can have a hugely positive impact on your mental wellbeing. Try to prioritize this in your daily life, if possible.

Chapter 5
Personal Health, Nature, and New Perspectives

Empaths typically find that they need to spend plenty of time alone to gather their thoughts. In fact, if they are forced to be around people for too long, it might even cause them to start feeling quite frazzled and disturbed, which is very obvious in empathy kids. They might get distracted or bored quite easily if they aren't in a stimulating environment, since they have a rich inner-world that they can retreat to any time and doodle or daydream. When an empath enjoys what they are doing, they are very dedicated, enthusiastic, and hardworking, but trying to get them to do an activity they don't want to do usually won't lead to much success.

Free Spirits seeking Knowledge and Answers:

The empathetic spirit loves to travel, enjoys freedom, and craves adventure. They are on a constant quest for new learning and knowledge, and love to find answers to their burning questions, whether they be philosophical ponderings or scientific. When they have an intuitive hunch, they love to find out whether it's correct or not. Routine, control, and rigid rules are the enemy of most empaths, who love to have spontaneous schedules. In the right environment and lifestyle, an empath is the happiest person you'll ever meet, but the opposite can be true if they are stifled or unaware of their own personality and gifts. Here are some more secrets for helping you reach your potential.

Secret Number Sixteen: Create a Welcoming and Safe Environment.

Similar to the tip in the last chapter about spending time alone, you must be able to do find a comfortable and safe place to recharge in order to recover faster and rebalance your mental and emotional energy levels. Environment is highly important, especially to an empath personality type. Although everyone may benefit from this, empaths do especially since they sense the vibe and purpose of spaces more than the average person. You can make this area your bathroom, bedroom, or anywhere else, but make sure it's your designated relaxation area.

Secret Number Seventeen: Make sure you Eat Healthy.

Many people underestimate the effect your diet has on your mental state. It may sound weird, but individuals who are in sync with their minds and healthy emotionally are less likely to crave junk food, and know that when they eat crappy food, they feel crappy. Instead, try sticking to food that is balanced and healthy, in your day to day diet. Mix in plenty of vegetables, fruits, and healthy lean meats like fish and chicken. Remember that the less processed the food is, the healthier it probably is. This is not to say that you can't enjoy treats every once in a while, but try to cut down on junk.

Secret Number Eighteen: Try out some Yoga.

Staying flexible and healthy can give you an extra activity to retreat to in the midst of stress, and being stronger is never a bad idea! Yoga helps to stretch out all of your main muscle groups and can help a lot with excess tension in the body. Here are some ways to get started:

- **YouTube:** We live in a time period where nearly anything you wish to learn is just a click away. Search YouTube for some beginner yoga videos and start learning now!

- **Take a Class:** If you have the free time (and in some cases, the money), try taking a beginner yoga class. Remember that everyone there is a beginner and there's nothing to be embarrassed about.

Secret Number Nineteen: Spend Time around Trees.

The link between empaths and nature has already been mentioned a couple of times, but trees are especially powerful. Get outside and look at and enjoy trees as often as you can. Even a short amount of time surrounded by trees can boost your mental and emotional energy and mood. If you have a busy schedule that doesn't allow for this as often as you'd like, try looking at some photos of trees, or drawing them at work.

Secret Number Twenty: Shift your Perspectives on Energy and People.

Empaths can find it hard to experience and witness other people. You have an overabundance of kindness and caring, in most cases, so when people are acting negative toward each other, it can be extremely disturbing to you and your peace of mind.

- **Relabeling Judgments:** It's easy to see someone acting mean and automatically assume that they are evil or bad, but try instead to see that they are probably just hurting or misguided.

- **See their Past:** It becomes easier to have compassion on people when we see them as people who didn't get enough love when they were children or people who have been hurt repeatedly and hardened themselves as a defense mechanism.

When you decide to shift your perspective of energies and the people behind them, you automatically minimize the effect these factors have on you with a deeper understanding and awareness. You might notice that you feel sympathy or even love for these people where you once only felt frustration or anger.

The Fear around being an Empath and Digging Deeper:

Unfortunately, the concept of having the personality of an empath is surrounded by fear. As soon as you begin looking up this phenomenon, you will find lots of information about shutting other people out of your life in order to protect yourself, or being generally mistrustful of people. Although protection is important, and shielding is a valuable skill for an empath, it becomes a lot less necessary when you realize that you don't have an obligation to take on the troubles of other people.

Reasons to use the "Shielding" Technique Sparingly and Carefully:

It's important to know how to keep yourself safe from harm and the mental baggage of others, but there are a few reasons why this technique should be used wisely.

- **It can lead to inner Conflict:** This technique, when used wrongly, can lead to turmoil inside of you. Although it's a useful temporary measure, it isn't a permanent cure for energy drain and the feeling of being overwhelmed around people. In addition to this, it's a way to put off examining methods for understanding why you absorb people's energy so easily, and finding healthy coping mechanisms for that.

- **Use Observation:** For those reasons, it's a better idea to pay attention to what emotions and beliefs in our minds are influencing the dynamics going on between us and other people. Become focused on your own inner world to gain understanding. When you take on a willingness to do this, you get control over yourself and your personal moods and energies.

- **Why "should" you be around Negative Influences?** You can start by paying attention to the reasons you think you should spend time with those who impact you in a negative way. This could be guilt, a sense of obligation, or some long term attachment to a particular person. If this is the case, your shielding strategies and techniques will not go very far. Oftentimes, beliefs like this have roots that stretch far back into our pasts, and could be linked to our parents or another influential authority figure from the past.

- **Do you feel a Responsibility for Others' Emotions?** Whether you do or not, you are causing yourself a lot of unnecessary suffering if you don't evaluate these tendencies within yourself. Think about the mental energy you put into shielding yourself from negativity, when it could simply be avoided in the first place. Be honest with yourself about what needs to change within you, versus what should change in your environment.

When you start to look into your emotional habits, thought patterns, and roles from the past, it can lead to a lot of resistance within yourself. But this will help you gain control over your own sensitivity, instead of feeling tossed about by outside influences in your life, and isn't that the ultimate ideal of every empath?

Chapter 6

Gratefulness, Boundaries, and Personal Responsibility

When you're an empath, you find that people almost instinctively want to dump their problems onto you. This is because they can sense your openness and understanding and gravitate towards you for this reason, wanting to bare their souls to someone who can see their emotions. For this reason, it's easy to constantly feel tired and overwhelmed. Your energy can be drained easily simply from being around other people or listening to their problems too much. All of this is fine and can even be healthy for you, but only when you know how to properly handle such situations.

This can lead to some dangerous situations for you. When you aren't equipped to deal with your personality and set boundaries for yourself with other people, you might find yourself very anxious or depressed quite often. You may even find yourself drawn to drugs, sex, or alcohol in order to distract yourself from these uncomfortable feelings. This is an understandable instinct toward protecting yourself, but it only masks the problem and makes it harder to fix.

Your Gifts for Creativity and Spirituality:

Empaths have a great gift for spiritual subjects and creativity, in general. You are drawn to holistic therapy, healing, and thinking about metaphysical subjects. For some empaths, healing comes naturally, but they end up denying this path because it becomes too overwhelming or painful to take on the baggage of other people. This is only a problem when the empath is not aware of their own gifts and how to wield them. When it comes to supernatural subjects, the empath is not easily surprised or shocked, only interested and intrigued.

Finding a Creative Outlet as an Empath:

Whether your calling is writing, drawing, dancing, or singing, as an empath you need an outlet for your creativity. You will find that your imagination is naturally vivid and that creativity is as instinctual to you as breathing, and this calling should never be denied. You may find yourself with a need to be around animals and nature often in order to stay sane and balanced, and to shy away from getting too absorbed in television or the news. If you aren't sure which creative activity you should pursue, you can try doing an online search to find out what calls to you.

Secret Number Twenty One: Getting in touch with Spirituality.

As mentioned above, you have a natural inclination for spirituality, but existing in our hardened world can dull that natural proclivity. For this reason, it's important to get back to your nature as an empath.

- **Praying:** You might be religious, or you might not, but praying can be a very general activity and not necessarily directed at a particular god. You could pray to your guardian angels, the universe, or even your higher self. It's a very calming activity that can help you get a grip when life gets overwhelming. Even if it doesn't seem like it's your thing, it might be worth a shot.

- **Stones or Crystals:** Some people feel very strong energetic connections with gemstones or crystals. If you haven't ever found out about this, it's worth buying some to try it out; they can be found online or in local shops for very affordable prices. Some find that carrying them around is helpful, or even making them into jewelry.

- **Chakra Cleansing:** In ancient tradition, chakras are known as your energetic and spiritual centers. An effective and popular method for cleansing these energetic centers is using aromatherapy. This can be done with scented oils or even scented candles. Some find that this is extra effective when combined with prayer or meditation.

- **Being Thankful Every day:** Gratefulness is a habit that we cultivate, not something that comes to us automatically. It's a choice you make every day to look for the good in life and appreciate what you have and who you are. In order to make the most of your unique personality traits and gifts as an empath, start to cultivate a grateful attitude that searches for the inherent strengths in these abilities. Rather than constantly feeling sorry for who you are, try to instead own it and be proud.

How should you practice this new and unfamiliar habit of being grateful in your day to day life? Some find it helpful to start a journal that details their gratitude, an online blog, or simply saying what they are thankful for out loud each and every morning. Find the method that works for you and makes you happiest. This attitude change will transform your life with very minimal effort.

Secret Number Twenty Two: Recognize the Strength in your Gift.

Yes, I said your gift, because that's what being an empath really is. Although it does feel burdensome at times, you experience reality in a deeper way than most people, and that should never be taken for granted. Try to be grateful for what you have instead of wishing you were a different person. Creating a habit of being thankful is creating a momentum of positive energy that will change your life for the better.

Secret Number Twenty Three: Set Personal Boundaries for yourself.

All of us have individuals in our lives that unknowingly intrude into your bubble of energy without being aware of it. This is what makes it so important to establish boundaries where and when they're required. This can refer to temporal, conversational, or physical boundaries, all depending on how people invade your space. Make sure that you are always confident and firm in the limits you set for yourself. You deserve peace and happiness just as much as anyone else.

Secret Number Twenty Four: Always Take Personal Responsibility for yourself.

If you are under the belief that other people should change themselves to adjust to your ways of sensitivity, you will likely end up hurt and disappointed when it never happens. Rather, once you acknowledge your nature, start to be responsible for your personal wellbeing and state of mind, using the secrets and tips given to you in this book. Keep in mind that your personal joy and peace are creations that you, and no one else, are responsible for. Stay empowered, confident, and always believe in your own abilities to handle life.

Secret Number Twenty Five: Keep a Daily Journal.

This is one of the most important aspects of being an empath. You should journal to record significant events in your life, track how they made you feel, and keep tabs on your personal progress and goals. Write in it every day, even if it's only one paragraph or a few sentences. You will be amazed at the clarity it brings you. Here are some ideas for what to write about when you first get started:

- **The "Sponging" effect of the Empath:** Many societies believe that whatever a person feels is all about them and has nothing to do with other people. This would mean that the logical assumption to make is that all that you feel is coming from you. In your journal, try to note the strong feelings you had throughout your day and where you believe they came from. This will help you get into the habit of noticing your inner world and paying attention to what is happening inside you.

- **Finding Reasons for your Feelings:** Empaths like to reflect on themselves, perhaps a lot more than other people do. But if you find yourself analyzing every single mood you have and trying to find its source, you might get even more overwhelmed. Sometimes, it's okay to just feel something and let it go. In your journal, try to record examples of these type of scenarios, including how you handled it, how you wish to handle it better in the future, and more.

Using your Traits to your Advantage:

When you learn how to train yourself in your empathy, you acknowledge your innate gifts and find ways to use them in ways that are healthy for you. This includes habits of caring for yourself, and realizing that putting aside your own needs for others is not a good idea. Here is what it looks like to have this healthy perspective about your empath nature:

- **Neutrality toward Others' Emotions:** A trained, healthy, and experienced empath knows how to take a neutral stance and perspective in relation to the energy and emotion of other people. It doesn't mean that they don't still feel a lot and feel very deeply, but you are in control of what you allow to affect you and when to let it go.

- **Deciding how Long to feel it:** At times, as a trained and knowledgeable empath, you might decide to let someone's feelings and emotions into your mind for the sake of helping them out. This is fine, but it must be done in a balanced way in order to be healthy, and you have to be able to let it go when it's time in order to uphold your own mental wellbeing and personal emotions.

The struggle with being an empath is becoming the master of your own inner world, but with practice, it's very possible. If you follow the tips outlined in this book, you will soon find that the sensitivity that you once cursed and wished were gone is actually a wonderful strength. You will come to appreciate your personality traits and quirks, and feel proud of them instead of ashamed. Once you master this and control your sensitivity in a healthy manner, you can help others in amazing and incredible ways.

Conclusion

Thank you again for buying this book!

I hope this book was able to help you to realize that there is absolutely nothing wrong with you. In fact, being a highly empathetic person is a great skill to have, and you have much to teach others if you learn to acknowledge and accept yourself and your own innate gifts. Once you realize the amazing power you have within you, there is no limit to what you can do with it. Stop resisting yourself and start being grateful for who you are, and your life will transform before your eyes.

 The next step is to make sure that you are prioritizing your peace of mind, not letting others take advantage of you, and putting the tips given to you in this book into practice. With that information, it's only a matter of time before you can walk through life self-assured and confident, no matter what unexpected occurrences pop up.

Finally, if you enjoyed this book, then I'd like to ask you for a favor, would you be kind enough to leave a review for this book on Amazon? It'd be greatly appreciated!

Thank you and good luck!

Description

Do you find yourself constantly overwhelmed by stimuli outside of you, including loud noises, strong feelings of others, and your own thoughts and ideas? This book is for you. In this guide, you will learn:

- **What makes an Empath?** Is being an empath the same as being empathetic? Actually, it isn't. It's much more than that, and you'll find out exactly how. Even if you just tend to be more empathetic than others, you will find the information in this guide helpful for managing and navigating your emotions and the emotions of those around you.

- **How does one Protect themselves?** Once you realize that you feel deeply and that it's just a part of your personality, what do you do with that information? There are plenty of useful tips to learn that show you how to ground yourself in times of stress, not take things so personally, and recover quickly from overwhelming environments.

- **How should you find Peace in a Rowdy World?** A huge part of navigating life as this type of personality is making time for yourself, creating quiet space in your life, and a designated routine that allows you to connect with yourself on a regular basis.

Stop working against yourself and start loving yourself. Being an empath is actually a wonderful blessing when you know how to use it and shield yourself from unnecessary negativity. With the information given to you in this book, you can take yourself to the next level and experience the joy and happiness you truly deserve.

17515715R00039

Printed in Poland
by Amazon Fulfillment
Poland Sp. z o.o., Wrocław